TRINITY
COLLEGE LONDON

GW00363640

1 2 3 1 2 3 1
G A B C D E
5 4 3 2 1 3

+ Blk Chord fingering RH 1 3 5   3
LH 5 3 1   5 2 1 2

1 2 3 1 2 3 4 5
E F# G A B C D# E
5 4 3 2 1 3 2 1

Piano
Grade 1

D chromatic 1 3 1 2 3 1 3 1 3 1 2 3 1
contrary

Pieces & Exercises
for Trinity College London
examinations

1 2 3 4 1 2 3 4
F G A Bb C D E F
5 4 3 2 1 3 2 1

2012-2014

1 2 3 1 2 3b 4 5
D E F G A Bb C# D
5 4 3 2 1 3 2 1

Published by
Trinity College London

Registered Office:
4th floor, 89 Albert Embankment
London SE1 7TP UK

T +44 (0)20 7820 6100
F +44 (0)20 7820 6161
E music@trinitycollege.co.uk
www.trinitycollege.co.uk

Registered in the UK
Company no. 02683033
Charity no. 1014792

Printed in England by the Halstan Printing Group, Amersham, Bucks.

Gigue in G

Georg Philipp Telemann
(1681-1767)

Dynamics and articulation are editorial.

Menuett in F

from *Notebook for Nannerl*

collected by Leopold Mozart
(1719-1787)

3

Allegro in G

Carl Czerny
(1791-1857)

Allegretto

Franz Wohlfahrt
(1833-1884)

Our Old Stove is Bust Again

Traditional *arr*. Petr Eben
(1929-2007)

Saturday Stomp

Carol Barratt

The Very Vicious Velociraptor

Pauline Hall and Paul Drayton

Summer Swing

John Deh

Petit Mystère

Simone Plé
(1897-1986)

Composer's metronome mark ♩ = 60.

Gaik (Mayday Dance)

from *Melodie Ludowe*

Witold Lutosławski
(1913-1994)

Cat's Whiskers

Elissa Milne

Composer's metronome mark ♩ = 168.

Walking Together

Christopher Norton

Composer's metronome mark ♩. = *c.* 60.

Exercises

1a. Toast and Jam – tone, balance and voicing

1b. Two at a Time – tone, balance and voicing

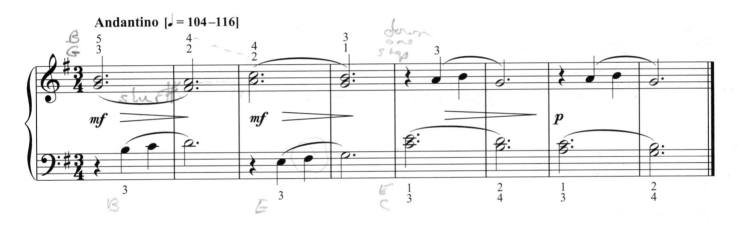

2a. Hill and Dale – co-ordination

2b. Scherzo – co-ordination

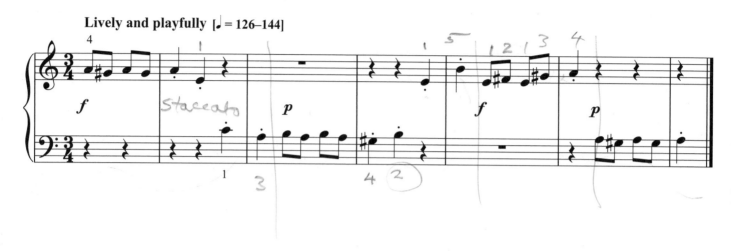

3a. Up and Under – finger & wrist strength and flexibility

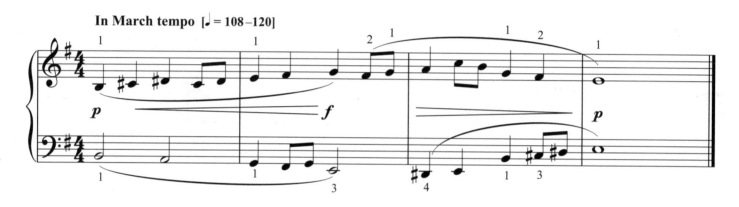

3b. Moving Out, Moving In – finger & wrist strength and flexibility

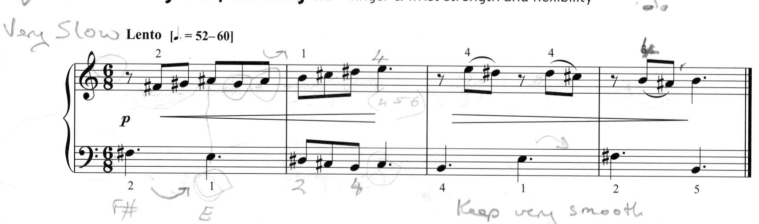